Spend It or Save It?

I0815343

BY KIM THOMPSON

A Little Honey Book

Tips for Teachers and Caregivers

This book supports early readers as they decode words to learn facts and gain knowledge about the world.

Before reading, make sure students understand the sound-spelling correspondences shown below as well as the high-frequency words shown on the next page. Introduce the vocabulary words.

During reading, provide feedback and encouragement as students sound out decodable words by blending individual sounds.

After reading, talk about and write about the topic. Share the information on page 16 to help students learn more.

Letters and Sounds

New:

consonant blends with *s*, including *scr, sk, sl, sn, sp, spl, st, str,* and *sw*

Review:

all consonant sounds and standard spellings; *short a* spelled *a*, *short e* spelled *e*, *short i* spelled *i*, *short o* spelled *o*, *short u* spelled *u*

Decodable Words

and, ask, at, bank, best, big, blast, but, cost, Dad, drink, dunk, dust, fast, felt, fest, get, got, gum, had, hat, help, in, it, list, mascot, must, not, on, pass, quest, red, rug, scrub, skip, slam, slip, slot, slurp, snacks, snag, specks, spend, spent, spin, split, stacks, step, sticks, stop, stress, stuck, stuff, swept, swim, tasks, ten, will

High-Frequency Words

New: could, much, said, so, then, want

Review: a, all, for, have, how, I, made, make, more, of, saw, the, there, to, too, was, water, with

Vocabulary Words

dollars

money

save

I was a big help.

I swept the rug. I had to scrub.

dollars

I got all the specks of dust.

I made ten **dollars**!

How will I spend it?

I want stacks of stuff!

“Not so fast,” said Dad.

“Stop and make a list.”

I made a list.

There was a snag.

It all cost too much.

I was stuck.

hat with mascot	$6.00
pass to swim at Water Fest	$25.00
Spin Quest	$3.00
sticks of gum	$2.00
red slurp drink	$2.00
	$38.00

I could not get the swim pass.

I could get the hat and the Spin Quest.

But then I must skip the snacks.

I felt stress.

? hat with mascot $6.00

~~pass to swim at Water Fest $25.00~~

? Spin Quest $3.00

sticks of gum $2.00

red slurp drink $2.00

$38.00

I could ask for more tasks.

Then, I could make more **money**.

I got it! I saw the best step.

I could split the dollars.

Slam dunk!

I spent $5.00 on a Spin Quest and a drink to slurp.

Then, I could slip $5.00 in the slot of the bank.

I will **save** to have a blast at Water Fest!

Build Background Knowledge

People trade their time and skills to earn money. Managing money involves difficult decisions. For most people, there is never enough money to pay for all they need and want. The benefit of buying one thing comes at the cost of losing others. Often, it is necessary to save money over time until there is enough for a larger purchase. How have you earned, spent, and saved money? How did you make decisions about your money?

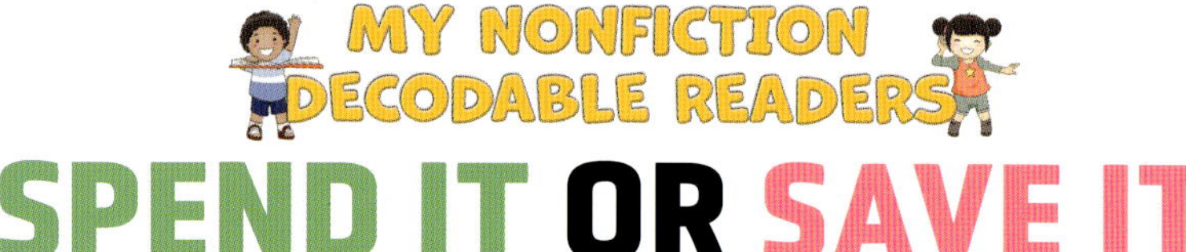

Written by: Kim Thompson
Designed by: Rhea Magaro
Series Development: James Earley
Educational Consultant: Marie Lemke, M.Ed.

Photographs: All images from Shutterstock

Crabtree Publishing

crabtreebooks.com 800-387-7650

Printed in China/012024/FE20231222

Published in Canada
Crabtree Publishing
616 Welland Ave.
St. Catharines, Ontario
L2M 5V6

Published in the United States
Crabtree Publishing
347 Fifth Ave
Suite 1402-145
New York, NY 10016

Library and Archives Canada Cataloguing in Publication
Available at Library and Archives Canada

Library of Congress Cataloging-in-Publication Data
Available at the Library of Congress

Hardcover: 978-1-0398-4437-7
Paperback: 978-1-0398-4518-3
Ebook (pdf): 978-1-0398-4595-4
Epub: 978-1-0398-4665-4
Read-Along: 978-1-0398-4735-4
Audio: 978-1-0398-4805-4